STRONGEST OF
THE LITTER

ALSO BY JAMES FRANCO

Palo Alto: Stories
The Dangerous Book Four Boys

STRONGEST OF
THE LITTER

A Chapbook

James Franco

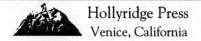
Hollyridge Press
Venice, California

Hollyridge Press
Venice, California
www.hollyridgepress.com

Cover Design by James Franco and Rio Smyth
Book Design by Rio Smyth
Cover Image by Miles Levy
Author photo by Anna Kooris
Manufactured in the United States of America by Lightning Source

ISBN-13: 978-0-9843100-5-0
ISBN-10: 0-9843100-5-3

20 19 18 17 16 15 14 13 12   10 9 8 7 6 5 4 3 2 1

Contents

STRONGEST OF THE LITTER

1. ELIZABETH TAYLOR

Grand dame, gorgon Martha
Versus your sliver tongued beau
Sir Richard as George.
That was the *later* you,

The you that passed through Cleo-
Patra, and brought down a studio;
The you that was James Dean's
Shoulder to cry on in *Giant*;

The young you that played Monty's lover
In *A Place in the Sun,* and his heart's support
In life. Could you comfort him
After his crash in the Hollywood hills,

When his face was readjusted
And he became frail and busted?
You climbed into the accordioned wreck
And pulled teeth from his throat.

Poor Monty, he became a shadow,
A slouched figure in too big pants.
You got big and drunk and weird,
You went on *General Hospital.*

Every once in a while they would drag you out
To give an award and you'd slobber on the mic.
But you were all those things from before
And all those versions of you, frozen on celluloid,

Especially in long lens close up,
Opposite Monty, at the dance,
So young and natural,
And that look right at the camera:

"I love . . . (gasp) are they watching us?"

2. MONTGOMERY CLIFT

You were the first.
Before Brando and Dean.
A new American way of
Fucking with the camera.

Your soul fluttered
Behind your stone still face,
A Donatello statue emanating
Deep life on the flickering film.

Burly Burt Lancaster feared you
Because of your latent power,
You played your character in
From Here to Eternity like a human

Knife in a Hawaiian shirt.
In *A Place in the Sun*, the longing
And sorrow and sociopathic
Intensity vibrate through

Your handsome mask.
Like nothing before or since
A minimalist artwork,
Motionless as it clobbers.

3. SEVENTH GRADE

A new school with cement all around
With wires that you can't see but feel,
And there are faces that break in at you,
And fill you with such pressure.
And you run away but the faces are always there,
Huge black ones that you never saw before,
On guys that are like grown men
That have dicks so big they could kill you.

But your dad says not to worry
Because if someone picks on you
You can handle anyone at that school, he says,
But he hasn't seen some of these guys
Because he himself wouldn't be able to handle them.
Gemal and Shaka and Ramone and Ruben,
They are different kinds of people than you have ever known.

The halls are full of these people and talk about pussy and guns
And a girl named Yvon that sucked Shaka's dick.
You try to picture it, and swallow that image whole, because it is new too,
But that world is unwieldy and can hurt you.

Instead, you have a bunch of mice at home.
That had started as two, but they fucked,
Then there were twenty little pink mice in the cage.
It smelled, and you sprayed it with Right Guard,
You separated the dad from the mom, so that it wouldn't happen again
But then the mom's belly got big again with more pink things
Because one of the babies fucked her.

Think of that son,
Half her size, with barely any hair,
Riding her from behind,
Not knowing why,
But doing it because he was the strongest of the litter.

4. WHEN I HIT THIRTY-FOUR

I looked around for love
And I knew by then
That love wasn't worship,
That love was ease.

Love was the smooth river
Of forgiveness that takes all
Obstacles, pollution and debris
(Love is of man, he sets the rules)

Pushes them downstream
And leaves them in the ocean.
I like the beer bottles that collect
Along the shore, the trash

From diaper boxes, and Clorox.
These are the rainbow colored
Punctuations stuck into nature,
They are the man-made things

Corroded by my love.
I assume things will pile
And pile until the piles
Take over. But sometimes

Things are washed clean
Like when a hurricane comes
Through and takes out houses
As if they were cardboard.

Love is not of man,
Nature sets the rules.
I've lived a life,
I've learned a few things

And this is a new lesson,
It says, *surrender.*

5. ART SCHOOL

The undergrads are fuckers,
Kids that do nothing
For their education.
They got in because they could draw.

When you're a young actor,
There are roles for young people
And it makes sense to act
At an age when your experience is limited.

But when you're an artist
You create the *thing*, and it shows
When your life hasn't yet been lived.
A bunch of bratty art about nothing.

•

Unless it has a frame.
Let me give you kids adult context
And I'll make your young passions
Ferment into great art.

There is nothing like the energy
Of the young. I thirst for it
Like a vampire. I use young people
Like they're oranges I'm squeezing

For my breakfast juice.

6. HISTORICAL

I used to think history
Was the truth
While fiction was made up.
But those history books

Back in school
Were put together
By marms and stodgers
That thought they knew

What was good to know.
But did you know
That many people in the states
Didn't know about the Jews

Killed in the holocaust
Until the 1960s?
Did you learn about
Anyone gay?

When something is taught
Something else isn't taught.
I grew up in the Bay Area
And was taught nothing

About Harvey Milk.
Who decided that?
That's like skipping
Martin Luther King.

7. WHALES

When I was young
I read *Moby Dick*.
I read it on the beach,
And I read it alone.

I wish I were Ishmael
Sailing with demons
On the high seas,
Pulling sperm from whales.

My favorite part
Is the beginning
When he and Queequeg
Sleep together and roam

Around Nantucket
And eat the best chowder
In just about the whole world.
In bed they cozy up together

A cannibal and a wayward
Young man.
Think of the sand
And the cozy heat

In those rough sheets.

8. FIFTH GRADE

It was an annual field trip, for which Mrs. Yount was famous,
That and that she didn't take bullshit.
And that she had cancer, and that she was black,
And said often, "Shut your mouth child," if you said something stupid.

On the ship trip, everyone was part of a different crew:
The rigging, or the bosun, or the fishing, or the deckhand.
We spent weeks preparing for our night on the ship,
What an amazing trip it would be.
I learned how to tie some knots,
I learned "starboard," "portside," "stern" and "bow,"
And the "capstan" and "galley" and "below deck" and all that stuff.

But what I really thought about was the coming night,
Everyone sleeping below deck, in hammocks:
If I could just sneak over to Amy Kush in the dark,
Then everything would be okay.

But her dad was Colonel Kush, a chaperone on the trip,
And what would I *do* if I did make it to that hammock unobserved
And lay down with her amidst all those other hammocks,
Low slung with bodies, like scrotums, no, like bells ready to clang.

And in the old days, back in 1850, what did all those sailors do,
Out on the sea for months and years.
There must be books on it.
There are also many books that were never written,
And think of all the stuff that could have been written in all those books
About what happened on all those ships,
And well, shit, we were just kids,
And just docked in the harbor, for just one night.

9. GAY NEW YORK

Gay New York
Is the name of a book
About Gays in New York.
From the 19th century on.

Back in the thirties
Before the Second World War,
Gay wasn't even a word,
Unless you meant happy.

You were "queer"
If you *acted* queer.
But you could turn a sailor
And still be straight.

As long as you didn't speak
With a lisp or wear a dress.
Funny how a concept can change
A whole culture.

We have to worry
About who we have sex with.
Weird how one little blowjob
Will make you a fag nowadays.

10. THEATER

A box with a stage.
The wall between audiences
And performers is as potent
And as invisible as ever.

It's funny, the setup:
Performing from a script,
Live actors recreating dead
Material. Scripts

Are what last.
Plays are recreations
Using real people to breathe
Life into the marks of the dead.

•

I make a living putting on masks
Of different kinds of people
And then animating them
With my own feelings.

Sometimes my feelings
Get the better of me and I forget
That my character is kissing
Another character and it's not *me*

Falling in love with an actress.
I like to blur the separation
Between life and theater.
Because I can.

I am a performer
And this is my text.

11. DOUBLE

Something scary:
There is a pair of twins
From Atlanta.
They're identical.

They've got hip-hop style
And chase ambulances
For a living.
But they want to be famous.

They're the same person
In two bodies.
They are never apart.
They sleep in the same bed,

Finish each other's sentences,
And share their women.
They like double penetration,
It's all they talk about.

At one point they were engaged
To a Penthouse model;
Only one would have been legal,
But they both would have kissed

Her at the wedding ceremony.

12. FLORIDA SEX SCENE

I've done fifteen years of movies.
I was once the young brooder,
The James Dean that made directors
Unhappy. I was more interested in me

Than in any movie I was in.
I didn't know that I was part
Of a bigger thing than just my role,
But now I know.

I'm the experienced actor now,
I am a teacher.
When I acted in *Spring Breakers*
My character was the teacher

And the young Spring Breakers
Were the students from hell,
The materialistic demons
From today's celebrity age.

•

The actresses were enthusiastic
And sweet, they were so happy
To be in a movie that critiqued
Their world, rather than added

One more layer of deadly bubble
Gum. When we did the ménage
À trois in the pool at midnight
The girls were drunk.

It was the sweetest thing.
They had taken shots in their trailer
Because it was their first sex scene.
In the pool we went at it.

And between takes, while they reset the lights
The beautiful blond one—
A realization of someone's dream—
Stayed in my arms and told me

Everything she loved about my work.

13. FAKE

There is a fake version of me
And he's the one that writes
These poems.
He has an attitude and swagger

That I don't have.
But on the page, this fake me
Is the me that speaks.
And this fake me is louder

Than the real me, and he
Is the one that everyone knows.
He's become the real me
Because everyone treats me

Like I'm the fake me.

14. MY NAME IS PATERSON

My father died in my Jesus year,
He was sixty three and I was thirty
Three. He'd managed a few things
And so have I. I drive a bus.

"Say it! No ideas but in things." Mr.
Williams has gone away
To rest and write and die. William
Carlos, your most famous line,

A *thing* in itself. I carve
These streets with my machine
And deepen the pathways
Like a child drawing over lines

Again and again, until the paper runs
Thin. Next to his famous dictum,
Mr. Williams wrote,
"Inside the bus one sees

His thoughts sitting and standing. His
Thoughts alight and scatter—" The bus!
The bus! Yes, these people speak for me,
I am a vessel holding all their thoughts,

A moving collage. Williams again—
"Who are these people (how complex
The mathematic) among whom I see myself."
I am a thing, and these people are parts

Of mything. Their exchanges, breaths and hearts
Buzz about my enclosure like blood
And the whole metal thing moves
Through the streets of Paterson.

15. PATERSON HISTORY

The history of my city
Is the history of me.
Like the bus route I drive,
A grid undergirds

Paterson with the past.
William Carlos Williams
Marked these streets,
Administering to his patients.

Young Ginsberg lived here,
Whose father was a poet
And whose mother went
Crazy. She was lobotomized.

When Ginsberg wrote "Howl"
Williams Carlos Williams
Became his new father.
I am a poet because I see.

There was a movie made here
Called *Far From Heaven*,
About a relationship between
A black man and a white woman

Made by Todd Haynes,
Self appointed son of Fassbinder,
The wild son of the Nazi generation
And purple melodrama of Douglas Sirk.

•

William Carlos Willaims tried to make
The Great Falls great
And *The Sopranos* made them
Terrible, by throwing a body

Over them. Both the Kantian
Sublime and as forgettable
As a Kibble's commercial.
There is a frame

Made by the windshield
Of my bus
Through which I see the world.
The passengers are my Greek choir.

So much hubris.

My bus is muscular;
A brontosaurus
With a tiny brain
That is me. Looking out.

16. MARLON BRANDO

I remember when I first watched
Brando in his wife-beater
And thought I had discovered him.
And then realized three generations

Had already succumbed to his power.
He has the strength of all that America
Has to offer from its art,
He is the bull and the ballerina.

I love Stanley Kowalski and Terry Malloy
Because they are the brutes
Puppeteered by a genius.
Instead of performances

They are manifestations of a wild mind
Wrestling with its crude incarnations.
Marlon Brando is man vs. nature
And that is what we want in a man.

Like Tennessee and Blanche
We want our poetic selves
Destroyed by handsome brutes
In wife-beaters and oiled hair,

The poetry of being fucked to death.

17. PATERSON LOVE

Love is a woman
Who does many things.
I don't laugh at her
Anymore, she's no fool.

You're the fool
If you think art comes from craft;
Art comes from framing,
Art comes from human imperfection.

I once wondered
If I would be like Flaubert and Joyce
Living with a person
Who would never understand his work.

Now I realize that I am understood
Only too well;
I'm a raging Kowalski whose
Temper can be measured by

How little I can give.
How abusive my reticence.
I wish I could turn
And be smacked

With an angel's wallop.
My wandering eye
Is glutted on the world,
But like William Friedkin

Said after filming fantastic
Landscapes in his failed film
Sorcerer, "Instead of nature,
I should have focused

On the landscape of the human face."

18. DE NIRO

There is a discipline
In young De Niro
That is so attractive
Because it is like Zen.

Travis Bickle and Jake LaMotta
Have such defined edges
They are sculptures
Mysterious as Michelangelo's David.

The roles were created
By a singleness of purpose
That is usually found in musical
Arts. Musicians disciplining

Their instruments and dancers
Working their bodies into submission.
Robert De Niro
Prepared like a physical monk.

He drove taxis and trained with boxers;
He went to Italy to learn Italian;
He gained eighty pounds.
Because of the intensity of the roles,

The man became a black hole.
How do you get to him
Except through the sharply etched
Performance as Corleone,

So indelible it's like a Durer etching;
Or through the bent antics of Rupert
Pupkin; his cracked smile a hint of insanity
That would resurface in *Goodfellas*

When he tells the guy that insulted Pesci,
"A little bit. You insulted him a little bit."
A dog smile before he stomped the man's head in.
I played his son once and watched every film

He ever did, the early De Palma things,
Bang the Drum Slowly, the Roger Corman
Ma Barker thing, *The Gang That Couldn't Shoot
Straight*. I fell in love with him on screen

Just like Sean Penn's generation did.
But the man seemed divorced from his
Old work, as if the Samurai that made
The Deer Hunter was dead.

Now he runs restaurants
And supports politicians and the kids
Know him as a comedic actor.
But I'll never forget Johnny Boy

In *Mean Streets*, he is a young De Niro
Never seen again.
He is so energetic and wild
How can you help but think

De Niro was giving us his youth.

19. BLUE BEING

There is a surface
That we all make together
And the wild man
Seems to pop through

Like a line dancer out of step
And others start complaining
That he doesn't know the moves
And he's stepping on everyone's toes.

There was a man named Mike
Who called my father five times a day.
You'd hear each burdened voice of the family
Shout across the house,

Daaad, it's Mike.

At dinner my father often explained
That Mike saw demons.
They spoke to him,
He thought they were real.

I pictured a flaming blue being
Entering the dingy room,
And sitting by Mike
On the gray sheeted bed.

20. ANIMALS

I am a cat man
Raised by cats.
I never had a dog
Don't know how

To walk them
Or play, or give
Them love, or clean
Up their shit.

My cats stay indoors
Because they live
In the city.
So they're nice

As hell
Because they don't
Need to fight
For their territory.

If I stayed in all of my life
I'd probably sleep all day too.
And only get up to eat
And chase my sister,

And gnaw her furry head.

21. DEATH

I used to say that no one
Significant I knew had died
But what was I thinking?
My first cat; my great grandfather;

My father's father,
But I hardly knew him
Because my father hated him;
He said he was a drunk.

I knew him from pictures
As a dark man with a beard.
And then my mother's father
And that was sad

Because he loved me so.
He was a surgeon
But all he wanted to do
Was paint and sketch.

Then my father passed
And that was a big one.
And I saw that all the motions
Of his life were sucked into his hole.

22. NOCTURNAL

I fight sleep like it's a sickness.
I work up my resistance.
I push it back as far as possible
Every night, like a runner,

Working down his time.
I run through books
And hike through films
And write like a sprinter.

I'm a nocturnal creature
And I'm here to cheat time.
You can see time and exhaustion
Taking pay from my face.

My poor face, carrying bags
Like luggage of a lifetime
And wrinkles like writing
In an ancient book.

In fifty years
My sleep will be death,
I'll go like the rest,
But I'll have played

All the games and all the roles.

23. TELEPHONE

In my parents' old bedroom
With the blue and white wallpaper
Of paisleys and flowers
There was a cream rotary phone.

I'd lie on the bed
That I used to lie on with my dad
As he'd pretend to steal my nose
—It was really just his thumb

Between his fingers—
I'd play with the phone,
Working the circle
Over the numbers

And forcing it back,
Slower than going forward.
My father's middle name
Was Eugene, but when I was young

I'd say "blue jeans." The phone
Was a toy until I had people to call.
One day area codes appeared.
So many numbers to remember.

Now you don't have to remember any.

CPSIA information can be obtained at www.ICGtesting.com
Printed in the USA
LVOW12s2222110214

373342LV00001B/287/P